mOOd Tracker

THIS JOURNAL

Belongs To:

____

____

____

Personal Data

Name : _______________________________________

Phone : _______________________________________

Address : _______________________________________

____

Incase of Emergency
Please Contact

Name : _______________________________________

Phone : _______________________________________

Address : _______________________________________

____

Essential Contacts

Doctor : _______________________________________

Pharmacy : _______________________________________

Eye Clinic : _______________________________________

Dentist : _______________________________________

Name : __________________	Name : __________________
Call : __________________	Call : __________________
Work : __________________	Work : __________________
Home : __________________	Home : __________________
Email : __________________	Email : __________________
Other : __________________	Other : __________________
Name : __________________	Name : __________________
Call : __________________	Call : __________________
Work : __________________	Work : __________________
Home : __________________	Home : __________________
Email : __________________	Email : __________________
Other : __________________	Other : __________________

m**OO**d Tracker

Date:

Food I Had today:

Things that happened today:

POSITIVE	NEUTRAL	NEGATIVE

Morning
Afternoon
Evening

Exercise & Activities:

After exercise I feel:

- ○ amazing
- ○ normal
- ○ tired
- ○ sensible
- ○ energetic
- ○ stressed
- ○ happy
- ○ sad

NOTE :

Notes

what I liked

what I did not liked

m😎😎d Tracker

Date:

😍 🙂 😀 😐 ☹️ Morning
😍 🙂 😀 😐 ☹️ Afternoon
😍 🙂 😀 😐 ☹️ Evening

Food I Had today:

Things that happened today:

POSITIVE	NEUTRAL	NEGATIVE

Exercise & Activities:

After exercise I feel:

○ amazing   ○ energetic
○ normal   ○ stressed
○ tired   ○ happy
○ sensible   ○ sad

NOTE :

Notes

what I liked

____

____

____

____

what I did not liked

____

____

____

____

mOOd Tracker

Date:

Food I Had today:

Morning
Afternoon
Evening

Things that happened today:

POSITIVE	NEUTRAL	NEGATIVE

Exercise & Activities:

After exercise I feel:

○ amazing   ○ energetic
○ normal   ○ stressed
○ tired   ○ happy
○ sensible   ○ sad

NOTE :

Notes

what I liked

what I did not liked

m**OO**d Tracker

Date:

Food I Had today:

☻☺☺😐☹ Morning

☻☺☺😐☹ Afternoon

☻☺☺😐☹ Evening

Things that happened today:

POSITIVE	NEUTRAL	NEGATIVE

Exercise & Activities:

After exercise I feel:

○ amazing ○ energetic

○ normal ○ stressed

○ tired ○ happy

○ sensible ○ sad

NOTE :

Notes

what I liked

what I did not liked

m**OO**d Tracker

Date: [ ]

Food I Had today:

😍 🙂 😐 🙁 ☹️ Morning
😍 🙂 😐 🙁 ☹️ Afternoon
😍 🙂 😐 🙁 ☹️ Evening

Things that happened today:

POSITIVE	NEUTRAL	NEGATIVE

Exercise & Activities:

After exercise I feel:

- ◯ amazing
- ◯ normal
- ◯ tired
- ◯ sensible
- ◯ energetic
- ◯ stressed
- ◯ happy
- ◯ sad

NOTE :

Notes

what I liked

what I did not liked

m**OO**d **Tracker**

Date: [ ]

Food I Had today:

☻ ☺ 😐 🙁 ☹ Morning

☻ ☺ 😐 🙁 ☹ Afternoon

☻ ☺ 😐 🙁 ☹ Evening

Things that happened today:

POSITIVE	NEUTRAL	NEGATIVE

Exercise & Activities:

After exercise I feel:

- ○ amazing
- ○ normal
- ○ tired
- ○ sensible
- ○ energetic
- ○ stressed
- ○ happy
- ○ sad

NOTE :

Notes

what I liked

what I did not liked

m**OO**d Tracker

Date:

Food I Had today:

Morning

Afternoon

Evening

Things that happened today:

POSITIVE	NEUTRAL	NEGATIVE

Exercise & Activities:

After exercise I feel:

- ○ amazing
- ○ normal
- ○ tired
- ○ sensible
- ○ energetic
- ○ stressed
- ○ happy
- ○ sad

NOTE :

Notes

what I liked

what I did not liked

m**OO**d **Tracker**

Date:

Food I Had today:

😍 😊 😀 😐 ☹️ Morning

😍 😊 😀 😐 ☹️ Afternoon

😍 😊 😀 😐 ☹️ Evening

Things that happened today:

POSITIVE	NEUTRAL	NEGATIVE

Exercise & Activities:

After exercise I feel:

- ◯ amazing
- ◯ normal
- ◯ tired
- ◯ sensible
- ◯ energetic
- ◯ stressed
- ◯ happy
- ◯ sad

NOTE :

Notes

what I liked
____
____
____
____

what I did not liked
____
____
____
____

m**OO**d Tracker

Date:

Food I Had today:

Morning
Afternoon
Evening

Things that happened today:

POSITIVE	NEUTRAL	NEGATIVE

Exercise & Activities:

After exercise I feel:

- ◯ amazing
- ◯ normal
- ◯ tired
- ◯ sensible
- ◯ energetic
- ◯ stressed
- ◯ happy
- ◯ sad

NOTE :

Notes

what I liked

what I did not liked

m**OO**d **Tracker**

Date:

Food I Had today:

☺ ☺ ☺ ☹ ☹ Morning

☺ ☺ ☺ ☹ ☹ Afternoon

☺ ☺ ☺ ☹ ☹ Evening

Things that happened today:

POSITIVE	NEUTRAL	NEGATIVE

Exercise & Activities:

After exercise I feel:

◯ amazing ◯ energetic

◯ normal ◯ stressed

◯ tired ◯ happy

◯ sensible ◯ sad

NOTE :

Notes

what I liked

what I did not liked

m**OO**d Tracker

Date:

😍 🙂 😐 😕 ☹ Morning

😍 🙂 😀 😕 ☹ Afternoon

😍 🙂 😀 😕 ☹ Evening

Food I Had today:

Things that happened today:

POSITIVE	NEUTRAL	NEGATIVE

Exercise & Activities:

After exercise I feel:

- ○ amazing
- ○ normal
- ○ tired
- ○ sensible
- ○ energetic
- ○ stressed
- ○ happy
- ○ sad

NOTE :

Notes

what I liked

what I did not liked

m**OO**d Tracker

Date: [　　　　　　]

Food I Had today:
[　　　　　　　　　　]

Morning
Afternoon
Evening

Things that happened today:

POSITIVE	NEUTRAL	NEGATIVE

Exercise & Activities:

[　　　　　　　　　　]

After exercise I feel:

- ◯ amazing
- ◯ normal
- ◯ tired
- ◯ sensible
- ◯ energetic
- ◯ stressed
- ◯ happy
- ◯ sad

NOTE :

____
____
____
____
____
____

Notes

what I liked

what I did not liked

m**OO**d Tracker

Date: ☐

Morning
☺ ☺ ☺ ☺ ☹

Afternoon
☺ ☺ ☺ ☺ ☹

Evening
☺ ☺ ☺ ☺ ☹

Food I Had today:

Things that happened today:

POSITIVE	NEUTRAL	NEGATIVE

Exercise & Activities:

After exercise I feel:

- ◯ amazing
- ◯ normal
- ◯ tired
- ◯ sensible
- ◯ energetic
- ◯ stressed
- ◯ happy
- ◯ sad

NOTE :

Notes

what I liked

what I did not liked

mOOd Tracker

Date: [   ]

Food I Had today:

[   ]

☺ ☺ ☺ ☺ ☹ Morning

☺ ☺ ☺ ☺ ☹ Afternoon

☺ ☺ ☺ ☺ ☹ Evening

Things that happened today:

POSITIVE	NEUTRAL	NEGATIVE

Exercise & Activities:

[   ]

After exercise I feel:

○ amazing   ○ energetic

○ normal   ○ stressed

○ tired   ○ happy

○ sensible   ○ sad

NOTE :

____
____
____
____
____
____

Notes

what I liked

what I did not liked

m**OO**d Tracker

Date:

Food I Had today:

😍 🙂 😐 😕 ☹️ Morning

😍 🙂 😐 😕 ☹️ Afternoon

😍 🙂 😐 😕 ☹️ Evening

Things that happened today:

POSITIVE	NEUTRAL	NEGATIVE

Exercise & Activities:

After exercise I feel:

- ○ amazing   ○ energetic
- ○ normal   ○ stressed
- ○ tired   ○ happy
- ○ sensible   ○ sad

NOTE :

Notes

what I liked

what I did not liked

m**OO**d Tracker

Date: ________

Food I Had today:

____

____

____

Morning

Afternoon

Evening

Things that happened today:

POSITIVE	NEUTRAL	NEGATIVE

Exercise & Activities:

After exercise I feel:

- ○ amazing
- ○ normal
- ○ tired
- ○ sensible
- ○ energetic
- ○ stressed
- ○ happy
- ○ sad

NOTE :

____

Notes

what I liked

____

____

____

____

what I did not liked

____

____

____

____

m**OO**d Tracker

Date: ____________

Food I Had today:

____

😍 🙂 😐 😑 ☹️ Morning
😍 🙂 😀 😑 ☹️ Afternoon
😍 🙂 😀 😑 ☹️ Evening

Things that happened today:

POSITIVE	NEUTRAL	NEGATIVE

Exercise & Activities:

After exercise I feel:

- ◯ amazing
- ◯ normal
- ◯ tired
- ◯ sensible
- ◯ energetic
- ◯ stressed
- ◯ happy
- ◯ sad

NOTE :

____

Notes

what I liked

____

____

____

____

what I did not liked

____

____

____

____

m**OO**d Tracker

Date: [ ]

Morning
Afternoon
Evening

Food I Had today:

Things that happened today:

POSITIVE	NEUTRAL	NEGATIVE

Exercise & Activities:

After exercise I feel:

- ◯ amazing
- ◯ normal
- ◯ tired
- ◯ sensible
- ◯ energetic
- ◯ stressed
- ◯ happy
- ◯ sad

NOTE :

Notes

what I liked

what I did not liked

m**OO**d Tracker

Date:

Food I Had today:

😍 🙂 😐 🙁 ☹️ Morning

😍 🙂 😀 😐 😫 Afternoon

😍 🙂 😀 🙁 ☹️ Evening

Things that happened today:

POSITIVE	NEUTRAL	NEGATIVE

Exercise & Activities:

After exercise I feel:

- ○ amazing
- ○ normal
- ○ tired
- ○ sensible
- ○ energetic
- ○ stressed
- ○ happy
- ○ sad

NOTE :

Notes

what I liked

____

____

____

____

what I did not liked

____

____

____

____

m**OO**d Tracker

Date: [　　　　　]

Food I Had today:

[　　　　　]

☻ ☺ 😀 😐 ☹ Morning

☻ ☺ 😀 😐 ☹ Afternoon

☻ ☺ 😀 😐 ☹ Evening

Things that happened today:

POSITIVE	NEUTRAL	NEGATIVE

Exercise & Activities:

[　　　　　]

After exercise I feel:

- ◯ amazing
- ◯ normal
- ◯ tired
- ◯ sensible
- ◯ energetic
- ◯ stressed
- ◯ happy
- ◯ sad

NOTE :

____
____
____
____
____
____

Notes

what I liked

what I did not liked

m**OO**d **Tracker**

Date: [ ]

Food I Had today:

| |
| |

Morning
😍 😊 😐 😕 ☹️

Afternoon
😍 😊 😐 😕 ☹️

Evening
😍 😊 😐 😕 ☹️

Things that happened today:

| POSITIVE | NEUTRAL | NEGATIVE |
| | | |

Exercise & Activities:

| |

After exercise I feel:

○ amazing   ○ energetic
○ normal   ○ stressed
○ tired   ○ happy
○ sensible   ○ sad

NOTE :

____
____
____
____
____
____

Notes

what I liked

what I did not liked

m**OO**d **Tracker**

Date: [ ]

😍 😊 🙂 😐 ☹️ Morning
😍 😊 🙂 😐 ☹️ Afternoon
😍 😊 😀 😐 ☹️ Evening

Food I Had today:

Things that happened today:

POSITIVE	NEUTRAL	NEGATIVE

Exercise & Activities:

After exercise I feel:

○ amazing   ○ energetic
○ normal   ○ stressed
○ tired   ○ happy
○ sensible   ○ sad

NOTE :

Notes

what I liked

what I did not liked

m**OO**d **Tracker**

Date: [____________]

Food I Had today:

[____________]

Morning
😍 🙂 😐 🙁 ☹️

Afternoon
😍 🙂 😐 🙁 ☹️

Evening
😍 🙂 😐 🙁 ☹️

Things that happened today:

POSITIVE	NEUTRAL	NEGATIVE

Exercise & Activities:

[____________]

After exercise I feel:

○ amazing   ○ energetic
○ normal   ○ stressed
○ tired   ○ happy
○ sensible   ○ sad

NOTE :

[____________]

Notes

what I liked

what I did not liked

m**OO**d Tracker

Date: [ ]

Food I Had today:

Morning

Afternoon

Evening

Things that happened today:

POSITIVE	NEUTRAL	NEGATIVE

Exercise & Activities:

After exercise I feel:

- ( ) amazing
- ( ) normal
- ( ) tired
- ( ) sensible
- ( ) energetic
- ( ) stressed
- ( ) happy
- ( ) sad

NOTE :

Notes

what I liked

____

____

____

____

what I did not liked

____

____

____

____

m**OO**d **Tracker**

Date:

😍 🙂 😐 😕 🙁 Morning
😍 🙂 😐 😕 🙁 Afternoon
😍 🙂 😐 😕 🙁 Evening

Food I Had today:

Things that happened today:

POSITIVE	NEUTRAL	NEGATIVE

Exercise & Activities:

After exercise I feel:

- ○ amazing
- ○ normal
- ○ tired
- ○ sensible
- ○ energetic
- ○ stressed
- ○ happy
- ○ sad

NOTE :

Notes

what I liked

____

____

____

____

what I did not liked

____

____

____

____

m**OO**d **Tracker**

Date:

Food I Had today:

😍 🙂 😀 😐 ☹️ Morning

😍 🙂 😀 😐 ☹️ Afternoon

😍 🙂 😀 😐 ☹️ Evening

Things that happened today:

POSITIVE	NEUTRAL	NEGATIVE

Exercise & Activities:

After exercise I feel:

- ⚪ amazing
- ⚪ normal
- ⚪ tired
- ⚪ sensible
- ⚪ energetic
- ⚪ stressed
- ⚪ happy
- ⚪ sad

NOTE :

Notes

what I liked

what I did not liked

m**OO**d **Tracker**

Date:

Food I Had today:

😍 🙂 😐 😕 ☹️ Morning
😍 🙂 😐 😕 ☹️ Afternoon
😍 🙂 😐 😕 ☹️ Evening

Things that happened today:

POSITIVE	NEUTRAL	NEGATIVE

Exercise & Activities:

After exercise I feel:

○ amazing   ○ energetic
○ normal   ○ stressed
○ tired   ○ happy
○ sensible   ○ sad

NOTE :

Notes

what I liked

what I did not liked

m**OO**d Tracker

Date:

Food I Had today:

Morning
Afternoon
Evening

Things that happened today:

POSITIVE	NEUTRAL	NEGATIVE

Exercise & Activities:

After exercise I feel:

- ◯ amazing
- ◯ normal
- ◯ tired
- ◯ sensible
- ◯ energetic
- ◯ stressed
- ◯ happy
- ◯ sad

NOTE :

Notes

what I liked

____

what I did not liked

____

m**OO**d Tracker

Date: ____________

Food I Had today:

____
____

😍 😊 🙂 😐 ☹️ Morning

😍 😊 🙂 😐 ☹️ Afternoon

😍 😊 🙂 😐 ☹️ Evening

Things that happened today:

POSITIVE	NEUTRAL	NEGATIVE

Exercise & Activities:

____

After exercise I feel:

- ◯ amazing
- ◯ normal
- ◯ tired
- ◯ sensible
- ◯ energetic
- ◯ stressed
- ◯ happy
- ◯ sad

NOTE :

____
____
____
____
____
____

Notes

what I liked

what I did not liked

m**OO**d Tracker

Date:

Food I Had today:

Things that happened today:

POSITIVE	NEUTRAL	NEGATIVE

Morning

Afternoon

Evening

Exercise & Activities:

After exercise I feel:

- ○ amazing
- ○ normal
- ○ tired
- ○ sensible
- ○ energetic
- ○ stressed
- ○ happy
- ○ sad

NOTE :

Notes

what I liked

what I did not liked

m**OO**d Tracker

Date:

Food I Had today:

Morning
Afternoon
Evening

Things that happened today:

POSITIVE	NEUTRAL	NEGATIVE

Exercise & Activities:

After exercise I feel:

- ◯ amazing
- ◯ normal
- ◯ tired
- ◯ sensible
- ◯ energetic
- ◯ stressed
- ◯ happy
- ◯ sad

NOTE :

Notes

what I liked

what I did not liked

m**OO**d Tracker

Date: [______]

Food I Had today:

[______]

😍 🙂 😐 🙁 ☹️ Morning

😍 🙂 😐 🙁 ☹️ Afternoon

😍 🙂 😐 🙁 ☹️ Evening

Things that happened today:

POSITIVE	NEUTRAL	NEGATIVE

Exercise & Activities:

[______]

After exercise I feel:

- ○ amazing
- ○ normal
- ○ tired
- ○ sensible
- ○ energetic
- ○ stressed
- ○ happy
- ○ sad

NOTE :

____
____
____
____
____
____

Notes

what I liked

what I did not liked

m**OO**d Tracker

Date: [ ]

Food I Had today:

____

____

😍 🙂 😐 😕 ☹ Morning

😍 🙂 😐 😕 ☹ Afternoon

😍 🙂 😐 😕 ☹ Evening

Things that happened today:

POSITIVE	NEUTRAL	NEGATIVE

Exercise & Activities:

After exercise I feel:

- ( ) amazing   ( ) energetic
- ( ) normal   ( ) stressed
- ( ) tired   ( ) happy
- ( ) sensible   ( ) sad

NOTE :

____

____

____

____

____

____

Notes

what I liked

what I did not liked

m**OO**d Tracker

Date: ____________

Food I Had today:

____
____
____

Morning

Afternoon

Evening

Things that happened today:

POSITIVE	NEUTRAL	NEGATIVE

Exercise & Activities:

After exercise I feel:

- ◯ amazing
- ◯ normal
- ◯ tired
- ◯ sensible
- ◯ energetic
- ◯ stressed
- ◯ happy
- ◯ sad

NOTE :

____
____
____
____
____
____
____

Notes

what I liked

what I did not liked

mOOd Tracker

Date:

Food I Had today:

😍 🙂 😀 😐 ☹️ Morning
😍 🙂 😀 😐 ☹️ Afternoon
😍 🙂 😀 😐 ☹️ Evening

Things that happened today:

POSITIVE	NEUTRAL	NEGATIVE

Exercise & Activities:

After exercise I feel:

- ⚪ amazing
- ⚪ normal
- ⚪ tired
- ⚪ sensible
- ⚪ energetic
- ⚪ stressed
- ⚪ happy
- ⚪ sad

NOTE :

Notes

what I liked

what I did not liked

mOOd Tracker

Date:

Food I Had today:

☻ ☺ ☺ ☺ ☹ Morning

☻ ☺ ☺ ☺ ☹ Afternoon

☻ ☺ ☺ ☺ ☹ Evening

Things that happened today:

POSITIVE	NEUTRAL	NEGATIVE

Exercise & Activities:

After exercise I feel:

- ◯ amazing
- ◯ normal
- ◯ tired
- ◯ sensible
- ◯ energetic
- ◯ stressed
- ◯ happy
- ◯ sad

NOTE :

Notes

what I liked

what I did not liked

mOOd Tracker

Date: ___________

Food I Had today:

____

____

____

☻ ☺ ☺ ☺ ☹ Morning

☻ ☺ ☺ ☺ ☹ Afternoon

☻ ☺ ☺ ☺ ☹ Evening

Things that happened today:

POSITIVE	NEUTRAL	NEGATIVE

Exercise & Activities:

____

After exercise I feel:

- ◯ amazing
- ◯ normal
- ◯ tired
- ◯ sensible
- ◯ energetic
- ◯ stressed
- ◯ happy
- ◯ sad

NOTE :

____

____

____

____

____

____

Notes

what I liked

what I did not liked

m**OO**d Tracker

Date:

Food I Had today:

☺ ☺ ☺ ☺ ☹ Morning

☺ ☺ ☺ ☺ ☹ Afternoon

☺ ☺ ☺ ☺ ☹ Evening

Things that happened today:

POSITIVE	NEUTRAL	NEGATIVE

Exercise & Activities:

After exercise I feel:

○ amazing ○ energetic

○ normal ○ stressed

○ tired ○ happy

○ sensible ○ sad

NOTE :

Notes

what I liked

what I did not liked

mOOd **Tracker**

Date: [ ]

Food I Had today:

☺ ☺ 😐 😕 ☹ Morning

☺ ☺ 😐 😕 ☹ Afternoon

☺ ☺ 😐 😕 ☹ Evening

Things that happened today:

POSITIVE	NEUTRAL	NEGATIVE

Exercise & Activities:

After exercise I feel:

○ amazing   ○ energetic

○ normal   ○ stressed

○ tired   ○ happy

○ sensible   ○ sad

NOTE :

Notes

what I liked

what I did not liked

m👀d Tracker

Date:

Food I Had today:

Morning

Afternoon

Evening

Things that happened today:

POSITIVE	NEUTRAL	NEGATIVE

Exercise & Activities:

After exercise I feel:

- ○ amazing
- ○ normal
- ○ tired
- ○ sensible
- ○ energetic
- ○ stressed
- ○ happy
- ○ sad

NOTE :

Notes

what I liked

____

____

____

____

what I did not liked

____

____

____

____

m**OO**d Tracker

Date: [ ]

Food I Had today:

[ ]

Morning

Afternoon

Evening

Things that happened today:

POSITIVE	NEUTRAL	NEGATIVE

Exercise & Activities:

[ ]

After exercise I feel:

- ◯ amazing
- ◯ normal
- ◯ tired
- ◯ sensible
- ◯ energetic
- ◯ stressed
- ◯ happy
- ◯ sad

NOTE :

Notes

what I liked

what I did not liked

m**OO**d **Tracker**

Date:

😍 🙂 😐 😕 ☹️ Morning
😍 🙂 😐 😕 ☹️ Afternoon
😍 🙂 😐 😕 ☹️ Evening

Food I Had today:

Things that happened today:

POSITIVE	NEUTRAL	NEGATIVE

Exercise & Activities:

After exercise I feel:

- ◯ amazing
- ◯ normal
- ◯ tired
- ◯ sensible
- ◯ energetic
- ◯ stressed
- ◯ happy
- ◯ sad

NOTE :

Notes

what I liked

what I did not liked

mOOd Tracker

Date:

Morning

Afternoon

Evening

Food I Had today:

Things that happened today:

POSITIVE	NEUTRAL	NEGATIVE

Exercise & Activities:

After exercise I feel:

- ○ amazing
- ○ normal
- ○ tired
- ○ sensible
- ○ energetic
- ○ stressed
- ○ happy
- ○ sad

NOTE :

Notes

what I liked

____

____

____

____

what I did not liked

____

____

____

____

m**OO**d Tracker

Date:

Food I Had today:

☺ ☺ ☺ ☺ ☹ Morning
☺ ☺ ☺ ☺ ☹ Afternoon
☺ ☺ ☺ ☺ ☹ Evening

Things that happened today:

POSITIVE	NEUTRAL	NEGATIVE

Exercise & Activities:

After exercise I feel:

○ amazing   ○ energetic
○ normal   ○ stressed
○ tired   ○ happy
○ sensible   ○ sad

NOTE :

Notes

what I liked

what I did not liked

m**OO**d Tracker

Date: ____________

😍 😊 🙂 😐 ☹️ Morning

😍 😊 🙂 😐 ☹️ Afternoon

😍 😊 🙂 😐 ☹️ Evening

Food I Had today:

____

Things that happened today:

POSITIVE	NEUTRAL	NEGATIVE

Exercise & Activities:

After exercise I feel:

- ○ amazing
- ○ normal
- ○ tired
- ○ sensible
- ○ energetic
- ○ stressed
- ○ happy
- ○ sad

NOTE :

____
____
____
____
____
____
____

Notes

what I liked

what I did not liked

m**OO**d **Tracker**

Date: [ ]

Food I Had today:

☻ ☺ 😐 😕 ☹ Morning

☻ ☺ 😐 😕 ☹ Afternoon

☻ ☺ 😐 😕 ☹ Evening

Things that happened today:

POSITIVE	NEUTRAL	NEGATIVE

Exercise & Activities:

After exercise I feel:

- ◯ amazing
- ◯ normal
- ◯ tired
- ◯ sensible
- ◯ energetic
- ◯ stressed
- ◯ happy
- ◯ sad

NOTE :

Notes

what I liked

____

____

____

____

what I did not liked

____

____

____

m**OO**d Tracker

Date: [ ]

Food I Had today:

😍 🙂 😀 😐 🙁 Morning

😍 🙂 😀 😐 🙁 Afternoon

😍 🙂 😀 😐 🙁 Evening

Things that happened today:

POSITIVE	NEUTRAL	NEGATIVE

Exercise & Activities:

After exercise I feel:

- ◯ amazing
- ◯ normal
- ◯ tired
- ◯ sensible
- ◯ energetic
- ◯ stressed
- ◯ happy
- ◯ sad

NOTE :

Notes

what I liked

what I did not liked

m**OO**d **Tracker**

Date:

😍 🙂 😐 ☹️ ☹️ Morning
😍 🙂 😀 😐 ☹️ Afternoon
😍 🙂 😀 😐 ☹️ Evening

Food I Had today:

Things that happened today:

POSITIVE	NEUTRAL	NEGATIVE

Exercise & Activities:

After exercise I feel:

○ amazing   ○ energetic
○ normal   ○ stressed
○ tired   ○ happy
○ sensible   ○ sad

NOTE :

Notes

what I liked

what I did not liked

m**OO**d Tracker

Date:

Morning
Afternoon
Evening

Food I Had today:

Things that happened today:

POSITIVE	NEUTRAL	NEGATIVE

Exercise & Activities:

After exercise I feel:

- ( ) amazing
- ( ) normal
- ( ) tired
- ( ) sensible
- ( ) energetic
- ( ) stressed
- ( ) happy
- ( ) sad

NOTE :

Notes

what I liked

____

____

____

____

what I did not liked

____

____

____

____

m**OO**d Tracker

Date: ____________

Food I Had today:

____
____
____

☻ ☺ ☺ ☹ ☹ Morning
☻ ☺ ☺ ☹ ☹ Afternoon
☻ ☺ ☺ ☹ ☹ Evening

Things that happened today:

POSITIVE	NEUTRAL	NEGATIVE

Exercise & Activities:

After exercise I feel:

- ◯ amazing
- ◯ normal
- ◯ tired
- ◯ sensible
- ◯ energetic
- ◯ stressed
- ◯ happy
- ◯ sad

NOTE :

____
____
____
____
____
____

Notes

what I liked

what I did not liked

m😍😍d Tracker

Date:

Food I Had today:

😍 🙂 🙂 😐 ☹️ Morning
😍 🙂 😀 😐 ☹️ Afternoon
😍 🙂 😀 😐 ☹️ Evening

Things that happened today:

POSITIVE	NEUTRAL	NEGATIVE

Exercise & Activities:

After exercise I feel:

○ amazing   ○ energetic
○ normal   ○ stressed
○ tired   ○ happy
○ sensible   ○ sad

NOTE :

Notes

what I liked

what I did not liked

m**OO**d Tracker

Date:

Food I Had today:

Things that happened today:

POSITIVE	NEUTRAL	NEGATIVE

Morning
Afternoon
Evening

Exercise & Activities:

After exercise I feel:

- ○ amazing
- ○ normal
- ○ tired
- ○ sensible
- ○ energetic
- ○ stressed
- ○ happy
- ○ sad

NOTE :

Notes

what I liked

what I did not liked

m**OO**d Tracker

Date:

Morning

Afternoon

Evening

Food I Had today:

Things that happened today:

POSITIVE	NEUTRAL	NEGATIVE

Exercise & Activities:

After exercise I feel:

- ○ amazing
- ○ normal
- ○ tired
- ○ sensible
- ○ energetic
- ○ stressed
- ○ happy
- ○ sad

NOTE :

Notes

what I liked

____

____

____

____

what I did not liked

____

____

____

mOOd Tracker

Date:

Food I Had today:

☻ ☺ ☺ ☺ ☹ Morning
☻ ☺ ☺ ☺ ☹ Afternoon
☻ ☺ ☺ ☺ ☹ Evening

Things that happened today:

POSITIVE	NEUTRAL	NEGATIVE

Exercise & Activities:

After exercise I feel:

- ◯ amazing
- ◯ normal
- ◯ tired
- ◯ sensible
- ◯ energetic
- ◯ stressed
- ◯ happy
- ◯ sad

NOTE :

Notes

what I liked

what I did not liked

m**OO**d **Tracker**

Date: [ ]

Food I Had today:

😍 😊 😐 🙁 ☹️ Morning

😍 😊 😐 🙁 ☹️ Afternoon

😍 😊 😐 🙁 ☹️ Evening

Things that happened today:

POSITIVE	NEUTRAL	NEGATIVE

Exercise & Activities:

After exercise I feel:

- ○ amazing
- ○ normal
- ○ tired
- ○ sensible
- ○ energetic
- ○ stressed
- ○ happy
- ○ sad

NOTE :

Notes

what I liked

what I did not liked

m**OO**d Tracker

Date:

Food I Had today:

☻ ☺ ☺ ☹ ☹ Morning

☻ ☺ ☺ ☹ ☹ Afternoon

☻ ☺ ☺ ☹ ☹ Evening

Things that happened today:

POSITIVE	NEUTRAL	NEGATIVE

Exercise & Activities:

After exercise I feel:

○ amazing   ○ energetic

○ normal   ○ stressed

○ tired   ○ happy

○ sensible ○ sad

NOTE :

Notes

what I liked

what I did not liked

m**OO**d Tracker

Date:

Food I Had today:

☻ ☺ ☺ ☺ ☹ Morning

☻ ☺ ☺ ☺ ☹ Afternoon

☻ ☺ ☺ ☺ ☹ Evening

Things that happened today:

POSITIVE	NEUTRAL	NEGATIVE

Exercise & Activities:

After exercise I feel:

◯ amazing   ◯ energetic

◯ normal   ◯ stressed

◯ tired   ◯ happy

◯ sensible   ◯ sad

NOTE :

Notes

what I liked

what I did not liked

m**OO**d Tracker

Date:

Food I Had today:

Morning

Afternoon

Evening

Things that happened today:

POSITIVE	NEUTRAL	NEGATIVE

Exercise & Activities:

After exercise I feel:

- ◯ amazing
- ◯ normal
- ◯ tired
- ◯ sensible
- ◯ energetic
- ◯ stressed
- ◯ happy
- ◯ sad

NOTE :

Notes

what I liked

____

____

____

____

what I did not liked

____

____

____